Skin Care Student Q and A

By

Deborah Schwabe

ISBN: 1-4116-8460-7

Thank you to my husband Paul and my family for always supporting me in each of my windswept choices that take me from one idea to the next.

For Dan and Joey, know that you can do anything you put your mind to. You are always in my heart and soul. Sometimes we need to look outside of the box to find the answers that are best for us.

Thank you to Debra Feindt for always believing in me. May you always find love and success in everything you do.

Thank you to the girls of Studio 7 for always making it fun!

Thank you to Pat Moore for giving us faith when we were searching for it.

Chapter 1, Products

Chapter 2, Skin

Chapter 3, Chemistry and Sanitation

Chapter 4, Facials and More

Chapter 5, Anatomy and Skin Disorders

Chapter 6, Make-up and Waxing Tips

Chapter 7, Peels and Microdermabrasion

Chapter 8, Licensing

Chapter 9, Extra information

Chapter 1

KNOW YOUR PRODUCTS

There are many different product lines to choose from and they all say something a little different. When you have learned basic product knowledge it will help you decide what you need or don't need from a product line. Explore different products, go to the store and turn containers over reading them. Do you recognize some of the ingredients on the back of the bottles? Look where an ingredient is on the list of ingredients. Is it near the top of the list or closer to the bottom? These are all things you will examine as you go through school. The more often you get into the habit of looking at different products and not just the product you use in school, the more comfortable you will feel.

Cleansers

What does a cleanser actually do?
 A cleanser works to break up the surface tension on your skin and remove make-up or debris that has accumulated on your skin. There are many different kinds of cleansers, and you will decide which one to use based on the client's skin type. You will learn about skin types and analysis a little bit later. Cleansers come in different forms, such as cleansing milks, foaming cleansers and gels.

What is cleansing milk?
Cleansing milk is a very emollient product. It is good for dry skin, dehydrated skin (yes, they are two different things, we will cover it later), mature skin, and sensitive skin. It is creamy in texture and usually will not foam.

What is a foaming cleanser?
A foaming cleanser lathers or foams when you move it around the skin's surface. Men tend to like a foaming cleanser. Many people associate the lather with a clean feeling. Cleansers do not need to foam to work.

What if I work somewhere that doesn't have a lot of different types of cleansers?

Each product line carries their own information on which product they feel would be most appropriate for different skin types. One of the best things you can do for yourself is learn ingredients and know what they do. You can then turn around any container and decipher what product would make a good choice for your client.

How do you decide which cleanser to use?

You decide on a cleanser based on the client's skin type. You will analyze their skin and then choose the appropriate cleanser. For more information on skin analysis, please visit that chapter.

How many times do you cleanse the skin?
The skin should be cleansed twice; once to remove the make-up or initial debris, and a second time to finish the cleansing.

What about make-up remover?
You may decide to use make-up remover. That is okay, but it is still beneficial to cleanse the skin twice.

There are so many ingredients in cleanser, how do I know which cleanser is a good cleanser?
You will learn about product knowledge and how to read labels in school. I can not emphasize enough how important cosmetic ingredient knowledge will be. Milady's has a wonderful Cosmetic Dictionary you can purchase through their website or many large book websites like Amazon or Barnes and Noble. It costs a little more than you may anticipate, but it will be one of the best purchases you will make during your time as a student. It will be a wonderful supplement to your learning process.

Toners, Tonics and Fresheners

What are there different types of toners, and what makes them different?

There are toners, tonics and fresheners. There alcohol content is what gives them a different name. They may be referred to as: toners, astringents, tonic fresheners or re-fresheners.

When do you use a toner?

A toner may be used at different times during a facial. A toner helps to remove residuals from the cleanser, can help restore the pH of the skin or can act as an antiseptic after extractions. Your teacher will direct you in the way that he/she wants you to use the toner, and during which step.

What is a toner actually used for?

A toner can act as an astringent, correct the pH after cleanser, and it will also help remove residual cleanser.

Can you skip the toner?

Toner is a recommended step when giving a facial. Not everybody chooses to use toner, but you should do as your teacher instructs you.

Exfoliation

What different types are there?
There are two kinds of exfoliants. Mechanical and chemical are the two types of exfoliants.

What is mechanical?
A mechanical exfoliants, like a scrub, you actually physically move around the skin and help to slough off the dead skin cells.

What is chemical exfoliation?
A chemical exfoliation like an enzyme or a stronger exfoliants like a peel work to break down the intercellular cement between the cells. They break apart the glue that holds them together.

Where exactly are enzymes?
Enzymes are proteins that can change things chemically. These enzymes eat and help to dissolve the dead skin.

What is gommage?
Gommage means to erase. This is an exfoliating product that you apply to the skin, let it start to dry, and then you roll it off of the skin. It comes off in little pieces.

What is a vegetal?
A vegetal is another name for gommage.

What if the client has sensitive skin?
A gentle exfoliant can be used with caution. Clients with sensitive skin also have dead skin cells that need to be removed, but you do not want to be overly aggressive.

How often should the client exfoliate during their home care?
A client can exfoliate 1x a week. Over exfoliation can sensitize the skin. A client with problem skin that is a bit thicker may be able to exfoliate 2x a week. Your teacher will direct you in this.

Masks

How do you decide which mask to you?
You decide based on client's immediate need and on their skin type. Many times you will use one mask, but sometimes you will choose to use two different masks on a client. You may choose to use a clay mask for the t-zone area while you are using a hydrating mask for the other areas of the face. You may also choose to use a paraffin mask as a second mask over another.

How long do you leave a mask on for?
Most masks remain on the skin from between 10-20 mins.

What can a mask do for a client? What are the benefits?
Each mask will have its own benefits based on the ingredients in the product.

Should a client mask at home between facials?
Yes! You will help the client decide on a good home care regime. Masking will be a part of this.

What can a mask do for a client?
A mask can tighten and tone the skin, draw out impurities, help clean up blemishes, hydrate the skin, sooth the skin and more. Remember the ingredients will determine the results.

How do I apply a mask?
You may apply a mask using either a brush or your hands.

Moisturizers

Does everyone need moisturizer?
Yes, everybody should use a moisturizer.
Many times a client with oily skin may be
concerned that it will cause problems. A
client with oily skin should choose an oil-
free product with non-comedogenic
ingredients. Remember that dehydration
and dry skin are two different things. A
client with oily skin can still be
dehydrated.

**What is the difference between
creams and lotions?**
Creams are heavier than lotions are.
Creams are a product that is water in oil
meaning there is more oil than water.
Lotions are oil in water. Meaning there is
more water than oil. Creams tend to be
heavier than lotions.

Sunscreens:

What is SPF?
SPF is the protection factor in the sunscreen. SPF ONLY relates to UVB rays or the "burning rays".

Does everyone need to wear sunscreen?
YES! YES! YES!

UVA/UVB rays- what is the difference?
UVA rays cause aging, while UVB rays cause burning.
UVA rays penetrate to the dermis of the skin, while UVB rays penetrate the epidermis.

Chapter 2

Skin Types

Different skin types, what are they?
There are three basic skin types and two "extras". Some people say there are "five" skin types. The three basic skin types are: dry, normal and oily. You will also see sensitive listed as a skin type and also combination. Different schools teach this different ways. Some see sensitive as a condition rather than a type, while other times you will see it classified as a skin type. Don't worry if you are taught one thing and then read another. Combination means more than one skin type. When you analyze the client's skin you will then determine what their skin type is. It is important that you follow what you are taught and what your text book teaches you. When you are further along, you can read different books and different theories on this and decide what you feel is the answer.
There is no right or wrong answer, unless you are taking a test. For a test, always answer the way you are taught in your textbook. Analyze the skin type first, and then consider the condition.

Skin type is genetic, a skin condition is not.

Skin types do not change. Conditions can change.

How do you tell them apart?
When you analyze the skin, you will look at tone and texture, tone and and pore size. Don't be afraid to touch the skin while analyzing it. You can check for tone and elasticity as well. You will look at the appearance and determine from what you are taught how to analyze the skin. In the beginning of this process it can seem overwhelming and you will wonder if you will ever be completely sure. It will become easier for you the more times you do it. You will gain more confidence in yourself the more you analyze skin.

What are the characteristics of normal skin?
Normal skin will appear smooth, plump with medium to fine pores. Normal skin will present with a more even color tone.

What are the characteristics of dry skin?

Dry skin will appear with small pores, a lack of sebum, and may be delicate and thin in appearance. Some people with dry skin may have a tight skinned appearance as well.

Dry skin vs. Dehydrated skin

Dry skin = lack of oil
Dehydrated skin = lack of water

What are the characteristics of oily skin?

Oily skin will show with larger pores, more sebum production, it may appear clogged, shiny or sometimes sallow.

What about sensitive skin or Rosacea?

Sensitive skin is a condition that has occurred to the skin, as is Rosacea. Sometimes a client causes sensitivities by using the wrong products or over exfoliating. Sensitive skin means reactive skin. Rosacea is a condition that affects the skin's vascular system. It can be sensitized skin and will need extra precautions. Remember that you can not DIAGNOSE Rosacea. Avoid fragrance, a lot of preservatives, extreme pH levels, and aggressive surfactants.

How many skin layers are there?

This depends on how technical you want to be. The answer can be 3 layers, 5 layers or 8 layers. When you see more layers, it means that one of the main layers has been broken down into more layers. For an example, you can say the epidermis is a layer, or you can say it has numerous layers in it. Again you will learn from your teacher and textbook what you should answer for tests. When reading other literature, be aware that you may see the layers listed differently and with a different number of layers then you were taught. It is not a right or wrong answer, it just may be more technical or less technical then you were taught.

Oil glands vs. Sweat glands

Oil gland = sebaceous gland

Sweat gland = sudoriferous gland

Oil glands attach and wrap around hair follicles.
A dead follicle means there is no oil gland attached to it.

Sweat glands go directly to the surface of the skin.
There are two kinds of sweat glands: Apocrine and Eccrine or Mericrine.

 Apocrine glands are in the underarms and pubic regions. They are active after puberty. The gland feeds into the hair and causes odor.

Eccrine or Mericrine glands go into the pores such as the forehead or palms. These are true sweat glands and respond to heat, exercise, fever and emotional stress. There is no odor associated with these and they secrete mostly water.

What is the "acid mantle" or "barrier function"?

Your acid mantle is the outer most layer of your skin combined of your sebum and sweat. This barrier protects from things such as bacteria and other invaders. The acid mantle's pH is between 4.5 and 6.2.

What is the Fitzpatrick Scale?

The Fitzpatrick Scale is a popular way of judging a skin's reaction to the sun. You do it based on how the skin would react without sun block.

Type 1- burns easily, never tans (Common with very fair, red hair, freckles)
Type 2- burns easily, will sometimes tan (Common with light hair, light eyes, blue, green or hazel)
Type 3- sometimes burns, gradually tans (Common, fair eyes, hair color varies)
Type 4- rarely burns, always tans (Common with Mediterranean's, some Caucasians)
Type 5- tans (Common with Middle Easterners)
Type 6- tans easily (Common with black skin)

Skin Care Analysis

The more you get to know skin, the more comfortable you will be with analysis. I remember trying to figure out what "congested skin" felt like. I had a moment in school where suddenly I understood, and yet couldn't describe the feeling to a fellow student, saying the much loathed "you will know it when you feel it". The more often you look at people's skin, the more it will come into focus for you! Remember pore size, texture and tone, and don't be afraid to touch it, to check for tone and elasticity. With a magnifying lamp, you will see a very close up view of the skin.

Analyzing skin helps you determine what you will do during the facial, which products to choose and what the expected outcome will be.

Skin simplified

Skin histology- study of the composition of tissue

Skin physiology- study of the functions of the skin

Healthy skin:
Smooth, moist and slightly acidic

Functions: Protection, sensations, heat regulation, excretion, secretion, and absorption

FYI:

Cells enlarge, flatten and bind together as they move to the top

UVB (burning) rays penetrate to lower epidermis

Biochemical reactions are still going on even though the top layer is mostly dead

You may see different layers called by different names! Become familiar with them.

Transepidermal Junction or Epidermal Dermal Junction-
The layer between the dermis and epidermis

● ●

EPIDERMIS LAYERS BROKEN DOWN:

Stratum Corneum:
Other names: Keratinized, outermost layer, exfoliated, scaly layer, cornified, stratified, Desquamasized, epithelial, horny layer, and dead layer
- no nucleus at this level!!!!
- 10-30 layers
- job: protection, to keep things out!

Stratum Lucidum:
Other names: clear, transparent, or fixed skin
- thick skin, but thin layer
- no organelles or nucleus
- only found on palms of hands and soles of feet
- desmosomes still here

Stratum Granulosum:
Other names: pigmented layer, granular layer
- 3-5 layers of flattened cells
- no cell division/mitosis
- intercellular cement
- polygonal/squamous shape
- acid mantle formed
- keratinization shows up here
- last live layer with nucleus
- job: protection, to keep things out!

Stratum Spinosum:
Other names: spiny layer, prickle cell layer, part of basal layer/or mucosum layer, stratum squamous
- keratinization STARTS here
- cells BECOMING polygonal
- langerhans cells
- desmosomes
- melanocytes reach up
- keratinocytes
- psoriasis thickens here

Stratum Germinativum:
Other names: basal layer, mucosum layer, deepest layer, birthing layer
- touch receptors
- merkle cells, meissner cells
- melanocytes
- pigmented

DERMIS:
Other names: Cutis or True Skin
- (1.5-4mm thick)
- Thickest layer, WATER STORED HERE, nutrients absorbed, vascular system
- COLLAGEN/ELASTIN, pain and touch receptors in this layer
- 2 layers: Papillary and Reticular (glands, hair follicles, looser density tissue)
- Hyaluronic acid- hydrating beneficial fluids found between the fibers in the reticular layer
- VITAMINS need to get to the dermis!

HYPODERMIS:
Other names: Subcutis, Fatty layer, Subcutaneous or Adipose
- Not on eyelids, shins, nipples, genitals (superficial fascia)
- Veins(venules) found here, arterioles

SKIN TURNOVER

Child- 7-10 days
Teen 2-3 weeks
Adult 25-30/45 days
(Average adult 1 month)

Lymph nodes- filter out bad stuff

Fibroblasts- cells that give birth to collagen and elastin

Langerhans cells- mostly found in epidermis, they stand guard and act as an immune response responding to antigens

Merkle cells- found in the epidermis, they respond to pressure

Meissner corpuscles are mostly found in the dermis and act as receptors to vibration and touch

Panician Corpuscles are concentrated in areas that are highly sensitive to touch; they are deep and react to vibration.

Chapter 3

Quick Chemistry Review

Organic chemistry- has carbon molecule, is living or has been alive, can burn
Inorganic chemistry- no carbon, non-living, can not burn

Matter comes in three forms: solid, liquid and gas

Atoms consist of protons, neutrons and electrons.
Protons are positively charged.
Electrons are negatively charged.
Neutrons are neutral.

Element- simplest form of matter
Atom- building blocks that make up elements
Molecule- 2 or more atoms

Elemental Molecules- 2 of the same atoms together
Compound Molecules- 2 different atoms together

<u>Compound</u>- chemically combined
<u>Mixture</u>- physically combined

Equal parts: acid + alkaline = neutralized
Forms water and salt!

Water is the universal solvent!

Cosmetic Chemistry

Miscible- liquids that can be mixed
Immiscible- liquids that do not mix
(Ex: water and oil)

Hydrophilic- water loving
Lipophilic- oil/fat loving

Non-comedogenic- less likely to cause
clogging of the pores

Hypo-allergenic- no fragrance, does not
guarantee no allergic reaction, but less
likely to cause

Fatty Acid- from plant oils and animal
fats (lubricating)
Fatty Alcohol- fatty acid + hydrogen
Fatty Esther- fatty acid + fatty alcohol =
Fatty Esther

Certified colors-(also known as lakes)
inorganic
Noncertified colors- organic

---

pH- potential hydrogen

Why do we want to manipulate the pH in skin care?
For better product penetration!

Functional ingredients- help products perform
Performance ingredients- help cause change

Carbomer- thickener and texturizer
Parabens- commonly used preservatives

Hydrator (also known as humectants) - draws water to the skin

Liposome- vehicle that dissolves into the skin
Polymers- vehicles that are time released (Also known as micro sponges)

Physical sunscreen- reflects the sun's rays
Chemical sunscreen- absorb and neutralize UV rays

Germs, germs, germs

What are the three levels of contamination?
Sanitation- reduces the number of germs
Disinfection- kills most germs but not spores
Sterilization- kills all germs, including spores

What are bacteria?
Bacteria are germs, or one celled microorganisms.
Bacteria can be either pathogenic or nonpathogenic

What do Pathogenic and Nonpathogenic mean?
Pathogenic- harmful
Nonpathogenic- non-harmful
*note- most bacteria are nonpathogenic

What about a virus?
Virus are small microorganisms that can even effect bacteria! They are smaller than bacteria. They are considered "submicroscopic".

What is one of the main differences between bacteria and a virus?
Bacteria can live alone
A virus needs a living host

What are Universal Precautions?
It is a set of guidelines by the CDC (Center of Disease Control) that assumes all blood and bodily fluid is infected. You should treat it as such!

Remember, the body's first line of defense is unbroken skin!

What is an MSDS sheet?
MSDS is an abbreviation for Material Data Safety Sheet. Each product has a sheet that describes proper use, active ingredients and safety precautions.

Chapter 4

Facials

Facials are the main part of what an esthetician does. An esthetician may also do waxing, make-up application and body treatments based on what your state licensing board deems is in your scope of practice. Each state sets its own rules and regulations and it is your responsibility to know what your state guidelines are.

Before you can do a facial, you should be familiar with the benefits, the skin, how to analyze the skin and the products you will be using. It is the esthetician who is trained to properly do a facial causing no harm, knowing contraindications, understanding how to use the products you have chosen, knowing the ingredients in them, how the skin may react to the products, and what the expected outcome will be.

The purpose of a facial is to help the skin stay healthful in appearance and also to work with some skin conditions to improve them.

Facials

Why are there so many different kinds of facials?
There are different things, conditions or areas that clients want to target. Some of these are acne, dehydration, wrinkles, and hyper pigmentation just to list a few. You can target the facial to help meet the client's needs and wants.

What is the difference between an express facial and a regular facial?
 An express facial does not include the full service, such as massage and extractions. A teen facial may be like an express facial, where it is an "introductory" and offers a deep cleansing, but does not offer extractions. Massage tends to be associated with a full facial.

What can a facial do?
A facial can offer a deep cleansing, help clean out pores, blackheads, and exfoliate, while re-hydrating the skin and more! You will learn to use the proper products for the facial you are doing, so you can adjust it to the client's wants and needs!

How do you decide what to do for your client?

After speaking with the client and analyzing the client's skin, you base your decision on the client's skin type and condition, along with the client's wants and needs.

What about a home care regime?

You will help the client with their product choices and recommend products that will help them with their personal goals. Some clients may be interested and follow your home care regime, while others may be happy with the routine they are currently following. It is your job to gently direct them towards what would be beneficial for their skin.

What about special skin conditions, such as Rosacea?

You would use products as you would a client with sensitive skin. Some product lines carry products for clients with Rosacea. We do not "treat" or "diagnose" Rosacea. If you feel the client may have something like this, you would refer them to a dermatologist or doctor. On the other hand, it is perfectly acceptable for a client with Rosacea to have a facial.

Is there anything different with a men's facial?

With a men's facial you will want to follow the growth of hair on the face. It will be uncomfortable for you to go against the hair growth. Normal patterns where you draw your hands up the face, you will want to adjust. You may also choose to use sponges rather than cotton so it doesn't get stuck on a man's beard growth.

Extractions

How do you know whether to extract or not?

If the comedone is open and you are able to extract it, you may do so. If it is cystic and painful for the client, you will avoid doing extractions.

Depending on your state board's rules and regulations, you may or may not be allowed to use a comedone extractor or a lancet. Know the rules and regulations of your state.

You may use your finger with finger cots on, or you may use small strips of damp cotton wrapped around your fingers. You may also choose to use cotton swabs.

When you are doing an extraction, you want to push down and in before extracting. Remember the direction of the pore openings while doing them as well. The nose and cheek have slanted pores while all others are perpendicular. And always remember to wear gloves!

It is important for the skin to be readied for extraction. You should steam the skin using either a steamer or a hot steam towel.

Comedone- a blackhead, sometimes referred to an open comedone

Closed Comedone- a comedone without an opening

Blackhead- a build up of sebum in a follicle that has been oxidized (skin and sebum, not dirt)

Whitehead- another name for milia, a closed comedone

Milia- small bits of hardened sebum under the skin, sometimes called a whitehead, looks like a small sesame seed at times

Follicular Debris- small pore that is not open enough to be a blackhead, it is more on the surface, you usually find this on the nose, and they look like itty bitty blackheads

What is folliculitis?
Folliculitis is ingrown hairs. When the hair gets trapped under the skin it can cause an infection.

Facial Massage

I remember when I started learning facial massage; I worried if I was doing it "right". You will find your own flow and pattern, but in the beginning, learn it as your teacher instructs. You are being taught specific ways to do a facial massage so that you can pass your state boards. Your instructor knows that they want to see certain procedures and steps during your state board testing.

Good massage may be a reason a client may return to you for future appointments. This is an area you want to excel at! Take your time and practice often!

It is important you learn each of the types of massage movements.

The five strokes you will need to learn are:

1. effleurage- light stroking, glides over skin, no attempt to move muscle masses

2. petrissage- kneading/writing or rolling motion, lifts muscle off of bone

3. <u>friction</u>- back and forth motion to warm up area, local or general

4. <u>vibration</u>- fine movement made by hand and fingers, "shakes the muscle"

5. <u>percussion or tapotement</u>- tapping motion, used when stimulation is desired,

What are some benefits of facial massage?
Increased circulation, relaxation, reduce stress, improve muscle tone, enhanced self-image, help to penetrate products more, decreases cellulite, and stimulate blood and lymph.

Are there certain types of conditions I shouldn't massage?
You do not want to massage inflamed skin, sunburned skin or on inflamed acne.

TIP:
Keep your nails short and neatly groomed.

Did you know...?

Massage means to touch, handle, knead, or squeeze or a "systematic manipulation of the body"

Mass means to press softly

(Mass**o** is Greek)
(Mass**a** is Latin)

Learning product ingredients

Product ingredient knowledge is key in your learning. You will be able to look at any product and know what it will do, and why. This may be the one of the most important things you learn during school. Take extra time on this section. It may seem overwhelming at first with so many ingredients, but it will make a world of difference.

Below you will find a list of some of the more common ingredients with very short basic descriptions.

Investing in the Milady's Cosmetic Ingredient book is well worth its weight in gold. Do be aware it is updated so try to get a recent copy.

Ingredients in cosmetics do many different things. They work to prevent damage from oxidation, hold products together, cleanse the skin, soften and smoothes the skin, give color or fragrance to a product, heal lubricate the skin, help spread products, carry other ingredients, heal the skin and act as preservatives.

Ingredient List:

Allantoin- soothing ingredient

Aloe Vera- soothing, healing abilities because it draws oxygen to the skin and holds it, cellular renewing, similar pH as the skin, and because its pH is the same as human skin,

Ascorbic Acid- the water-soluble form of Vitamin C

Ascorbyl palmitate- the fat-soluble form of Vitamin C, which is absorbed into the acid-mantle better than ascorbic acid

Bentonite- A naturally occurring clay Used in masks and foundation makeup

Benzyl Alcohol- helps clean the skin and kills bacteria; it also helps normalize the pH of a product.

Beta-Hydroxy Acid Peel – (also known as salicylic acid), used on acne and other conditions,

Bisabolol- A German chamomile, that is from flower heads. It is an anti-inflammatory.

Butylene Glycol- used as humectants and is resilient to humidity. It is used as a preservative and surfactant.

Camphor- antiseptic and analgesic, calms skin and reduces redness

Cetyl Alcohol- It is a surfactant and in hair products, while it is an emollient, emulsifier and thickener in skin care products.

Chamomile- an anti-inflammatory ingredient, soothes irritated skin

Coconut oil- is an emollient which helps spread product, as well as acting as a preservative

Comfrey- soothing agent, wound healing properties, anti-inflammatory

Cucumber- soothing, anti-inflammatory

Glucans-(beta-glucans)- help to soothe and moisturize the skin while reinforcing the protective mechanisms of the skin

Glycerin- used in many cosmetics, helps retain moisture, aids in plumping and helps dehydrated skin

Glycerol Stearate- emulsifier with skin conditioning benefits

Glycolic Acid- a type of AHA (alpha hydroxyl acids) Glycolic is one of the most commonly used acids for doing peels. This helps break down the dead layers of skin on the epidermis.

Green tea: antioxidant

Honey- antiseptic and good for dry skin

Hyaluronic Acid- Intensely hydrating, in all of our cells

Isopropyl Myristate –causes blackheads and is being removed from many products

Isopropyl Palmitate- binder and emollient

Kaolin- clay used to give color, and adjust powders, may also be found in clay masks

Lactic Acid- another Alpha-Hydroxy Acid AHA, that gently exfoliates

Lecithin- antioxidant, emollient, water binder, emulsifier

Licorice Root- Has anti-inflammatory properties.

Magnesium helps to remineralize and soothe the skin

Magnessium Abscorbyl - a stable form of Vitamin C which neutralizes free radicals.

Methylparaban- preservative

Octyl cocoate- surfactant used in soaps and other products

Octyl palmitate- thickening agent and emollient

Panthenol- water soluble vitamin B

Papain- An enzyme booster which is an enzyme extracted from papaya.

Phospholipids- used in cosmetics as emollients, binders and lubricants. They also draw water to the skin

 Propylene Glycol- Helps form the base of products.

Propylparaben- preservative that is less water soluble than methylparaben

Retinoic acid Vitamin A acid, may cause skin and sun sensitiveness, can also be used as an exfoliant.

Retinyl palmitate- Vitamin A

Salicylic acid- (see Beta-Hydroxy Acid)

Sea Algae- Moisturizing and anti-inflammatory

Shea butter- moisturizing and nourishing

Silicone- produces slip and richness. Used as a substitute for oil in many types of products.

Sodium laureth sulfate-surfactant for shampoos, too harsh for skin
.
Sodium lauryl sulfate- emulsifier, but can dry the skin, ok for shampoo use

Sorbitol - draws water to the skin, maintains moisture

Squalane- moisturizes, enhances barrier function

Stearic Acid- used as an emulsifier and emollient

Vitamin A- antioxidant, anti-aging ingredient

Vitamin C- antioxidant

Vitamin D-necessary fro building new skin cells

<u>Vitamin E</u>- cell renewal, anti-oxidant

<u>Witch Hazel</u>- helps sooth inflamed skin

<u>Zinc oxide</u>- sun blocking ingredient

_____

_____

Quick Facts...Did you know?

In 1902 Helena Rubenstein established the 1st beauty salon.

Cold Cream was the first modern cosmetic compound!

Esthetician and Aesthetician are both correct spellings!

Some states refer to an Esthetician as a Beauty Therapist, Cosmetician or a Skin Care Specialist!

In 1966 Christine Valmy opened the first esthetic school in the US.

Dermascope was the first Skin Care magazine for esthetics published in 1975!

Some products use Aloe Vera in place of water in their ingredients.

In 1952 the FDA banned ads and
misleading claims of products.

Utah is the first state to create two
esthetic licenses, a basic and a master.

_____

Chapter 5

Anatomy and Skin Disorders

Anatomy- study of the structures of the body

Physiology- study of the functions of the body

Know your Anatomy

This is the chapter that most people groan and moan about. There are a lot of muscles, nerves, bones, arteries and veins to memorize. It is your job to do just that!

It will make understanding your work much easier. Flashcards are a great study tool.

Below you will find a basic breakdown of the bones and muscles of the head and neck. When you become overwhelmed think of the massage therapist who has to know all the muscles in the **entire body**, then learning the muscles in the head and neck won't be so daunting!

One assignment that really helped me in class was to literally draw them out on a Styrofoam head. You can find one at the local beauty supply store for less than five dollars. These are the Styrofoam heads that you might put a wig on. You can draw right on them with markers. By drawing them out, it helped the learning process because I could see them, rather than just memorize them.

Another tip is placing your hands on your head or a friend while saying the name of the bone or muscle.

Be creative and you will find it isn't so overwhelming anymore.

_____

Here is an easy way to remember the systems in the body:

C-REMINDERS = each letter represents one of the systems

C- Circulatory
R- Respiratory
E- Endocrine
M- Muscular
I- Integument
N- Nervous
D- Digestive
E- Excretory
R- Reproductive
S- Skeletal

BONES of the Skull

Cranium- there are 8 bones connected by sutures or seams, 7 of the 8 are accessible
(8 bones= frontal, parietal-2, temporal-2, ethmoid, occipital, sphenoid)

Frontal- forms forehead roof of the skull, and upper portion of eye orbits

Parietal- (2) forms roof of cranium, forms sides of cranium

Temporal- (2) forms inferior sides of cranium and smaller portions of the cranium floor

Ethmoid- (1) between nasal and sphenoid bones

Sphenoid- (1) "butterfly shaped", forms middle part of base of cranium floor, only bone that touches all bones in the cranium

Occipital bone- posterior part of the cranium, forms base of cranium

---

<u>Bones of Face</u> –there are a total of 14 facial bones

(Nasal-2, Maxilla-2, Lacrimal-2, Palatine-2, Zygomatic-2, Inferior Nasal Conchae-2, Mandible-1, Vomer-1)

<u>Nasal</u>- forms bridge of nose, 2 fused together

<u>Vomer</u>- found between nostrils made up of cartilage and bone

<u>Maxilla</u>- upper portion of jawbone, forms center of face and inferior orbit of eyes,

<u>Lacrimal</u>- smallest bone of face, size of fingernail, forms medial wall, orbit of eye

<u>Palatine Bone</u>- L-shaped bone, forms, posterior form of palate, 2 bilateral

<u>Inferior Nasal Conchae</u>- forms lateral wall of nasal cavity

<u>Zygomatic</u>- 2 , cheek bone, temporal forms other part, forms cheek and lateral orbits of eyes

<u>Mandible</u>- lower portion of jaw, largest of facial bones, forms chin

---

MUSCLES

Orbicularis occuli-(2) around the eye
Action= close/squint your eye, depresses upper lid, elevates lower lid

Orbicularis oris- around your mouth
Action= enables you to close lips, draws angle of mouth medially

Zygomaticus-(2) zygomatic bone to the corner of y our mouth
Action= smile muscle, elevates the angle, draws mouth laterally

Buccinator- runs horizontally in cheek, forms main portion of cheek
Action= allows you to suck andblow, aids in chewing

Platysma- anterior portion of neck, large muscle
Action= pulls angle of mouth down, tightens fascia of neck

Occipitalis: works as antagonist to the frontalis
Action= retracts posteriorly allowing frontalis to work better

Frontalis: works as agonist to the occipitalis
Action= raise eyebrows and wrinkles forehead

Epicranius: another word for occipital-frontalis, covers the top of the skull

Temporalis (2) runs behind eye to behind ear
Action= helps retract mandible

Masseter- thick muscle, **one of the strongest muscles of the body,** Action= bilaterally opens & closes the mouth

Lesions and Skin Disorders

It is important for you to know when to refer a client to a doctor. There are some great sites on the internet that provide a wonderful assortment of pictures. In the back of the book there will be a list of some websites that offer photos for you to see.

Lesions come in different shapes and different sizes. They may be elevated or they may be flat. They may be related to the vascular system.

A lesion is basically a mark or abnormality on the skin.

Objective- what you can see, visible symptoms (example: redness, pustules)
Subjective- what the client feels, but can not be observed (example: itching, burning)

Benign- NOT cancerous
Malignant- Cancerous lesion

LESIONS		
Word	**Similar to**	**Characteristics**
Pustule	Papule	Inflamed, white/ yellow center, infected pimple
Bulla Vesicle	Blister	Fluid filled sac watery fluid
Furuncle	Boil	Subcutaneous abscess has pus
1.Petichiae (blood spots) 2.Telangiectasia (capillaries) 3.Cherry Angiomas (Raised red)	Vascular Macule	Blood seen under the surface
1.Ecchymosis 2. Purpura 3. Hematoma	Bruises	Collection of blood under the skin
1. Cyst 2. Turbercle 3. Tumor 4. Nodule	Hard Lumps	Solid, elevated bump, below skin, fluid or matter filled

Wheal	Hive Insect bite Uticaria	Itchy, swollen lesion, can be allergic reaction
1. Crust 2. Scale	Scabs and dandruff	Flaky, epidermal cells, sebum and pus may occur
Excoriation and Acne Excoriation	Sores and abrasions	Caused by scraping or scratching
1. Keliod 2. Scar	Overproduction of cells	Formed after injury/lesion has healed, Overproduction of collagen & fibrous tissue
Fissure	Chapped lips	Dry cracked skin, an opening in the skin to the dermis

Disorders and Diseases:

Disorder		Characteristics
Dermatitis	Atopic (hereditary) Contact (allergy) Chemical substance)	Inflammation of the skin
Dermatitis	Eczema	Painful itching disease with dry or moist lesions
	Psoriasis	White silver scales
	Perioral	Caused by toothpaste ,an acne like condition around mouth, itching and scaling can occur

Sebacious Oil Gland disorders	Acne	Chronic inflammatory skin disorder
	Cystic Acne	Deep pockets of infection, Inflamed pus or filled papules
	Comedones	Blackheads, dead skin that's oxidized
	Milia	Whiteheads
	Acne Cosmetica	Acne worsened by cosmetics
	Premenstrual	Related to hormones

Contagious Diseases	Herpes Simplex 1	Cold sores
	Herpes Simples 2	Genital herpes
	Herpes Zoster	Adult Chicken pox, Shingles
	Tinea	Fungal Infection
	Tinea Corpis	(Athletes Foot), yeast infection
	Tinea Vascolor	hyper pigmentati on or white patches

	Impitego	Bacterial Infection, most often in kids, clusters of small blisters or crusty lesions
	Verruca	Wart
	Conjunctivitis	Bacterial, crusty discharge occurs in the eye, Pink Eye

Non Contagious Diseases		
Autoimmune Disease	HIV	Autoimmune disease
	Lupus	Systemic condition signified by butterfly rash
	Disquoid Lupus	Affects skin & red patches around follicles, rash on face & back of arms

	Dermatomyositis	Effects muscles, characterized by lavender ring around the eyes, heliotrope shape
	Scleraderma	Thickening of the skin, appears on face and fingers and affects internal organs
Hyperpigmentation disorder	Chloasma	Liver spots
	Litigenes	Freckles
	Melasma	Pregnancy mask
	Nevus	Birth mark or mole

	Stain	Brown or white discoloration
	Tan	Overproduction of melanin --> UV rays
Hypopigmentation Disorder	Albinism	Absence of melanin pigment
	Hypopigmentation	Lack of pigment
	Leukoderma	Abnormal light patches and is congenital that destroys melanocytes
	Vitiligo	White spots on areas of the skin

	Vertineus	Fungal infection causes lack of pigmentation
Skin Cancers	Basal Cell Carcinoma	Most common, least severe, light pearly nodules
	Squamous Cell Carcinoma	More serious, scaly red papules or nodules, may get crusty layer
	Malignant Melanoma	Most serious, black dark patches, uneven in texture, raised

Rosacea		Chronic congestion primarily on the cheeks and nose, characterized by redness, dilation of blood vessels and severe cases papules and pustules

ABC's of Skin Cancer

A-Asymmetrical
B-Border
C-Color
D-Diameter

Acne

There are different grades or type of acne and as an esthetician it is your responsibility to understand them and know which types of acne you can work with. You will also want to notate on your client's chart their acne conditions.

Grade 1- minor breakouts with only a few papules or pustules

Grade 2- many pustules and papules

Grade 3- inflamed and red skin, many breakouts, may look like it hurts

Grade 4- cystic acne, looks painful, may have inflammation and scarring as well

You should not do extractions on a client with Grade 4 acne, and you should use your judgment and be very careful on a client with Grade 3 acne.

P. acne bacteria or Probpionbacterium acne is the name of the bacteria that causes acne vulgaris.

Chapter 6

Make-up and Quick Tips on Waxing

Make-up

Make-up application or artistry is also a part of the esthetician's license. Make-up application can also be used to help clients who need camouflaging. Whether you client is seeking a new look, getting a make-up application for a special occasion or looking to cover flaws, you will be ready to help your client!

Sometimes you can offer a client the opportunity to try something different than their normal routine. Stepping outside of their regular routine can freshen up a client's look. To know what colors would be complimentary to a client and work well, it is important to understand color theory.

You will also do a consultation with your client asking them their wants and desires. If they are used to a natural look, you don't want them to look like a disco dancer! What are their expectations? Are they here to get ideas for a special occasion? If they have had their make-up applied professionally before, what did they like or dislike about it?

Color Theory

Primary colors= red, blue, yellow
(No colors combined can create these)

Secondary colors= orange, green and violet
(The combination of two primary colors)

Tertiary colors= yellow-orange, yellow-green, blue-green blue-violet, red-violet red-orange, yellow-orange
(Combination of a primary color and a secondary color)

Hue- how intense a color is (purest form)

Tint- white added to a color, ex: pastel

Shade- black added to a color

Tone- grey added to a color

Neutral- equal amounts of warm and cool

Make-up Application Tips

- when doing make-up application, you start at the top of the face and work your way down
- lavender counteracts white
- a great surface makes for a better application, make sure the client's skin is moisturized or primed
- take lip stick from the side of the tube, not the top
- yellow helps counteract purple
- red helps counteract green
- concealer can be used over or under make-up
- if a person flinches, have the client blink next to the mascara wand
- after cleaning your brushes, store it with the bristles down so water doesn't get into the ferrel of the brush
- powder blush should be used with powder foundation or base
- cream blush should be used with cream or liquid foundation or base
- if a lip color is not the right color, try a lip gloss over it, or some gold eye shadow
- too light of a foundation may look chalky, better to go darker than lighter if you can't find a perfect match, but be careful because too dark can look fake

- you can test lipstick colors on the back of your hand
- practice on friends and family members
- when selecting colors take into account the clients complexion tone, do they have a cool or warm complexion, as well as their eye color and hair color
- application will go much smoother if you are prepared and have everything you need together in one place
- sponges are great for blending foundation

* A chance to make a difference:

When you are a licensed and trained professional, a great opportunity to share your experience is with the "Look Good... Feel Better" organization. This is a program that lets licensed cosmetologists and estheticians teach hands-on make-up techniques and skin care to cancer patients.

You can learn more about them at: www.lookgoodfeelbetter.org

Foundation- evens skin tone and helps cover imperfections

Foundations can come in different types, whether they are water based or oil-free, cream or liquid based. Creams offer heavier coverage, while liquids offer sheer or medium coverage.

Concealer- offer coverage to "conceal" imperfections

Concealer can be applied either on top of foundation or under it

There are concealers that offer minimal coverage and concealer that offers maximum coverage. There are numerous types available, be familiar with the many different types to get the right coverage for your client.

Face Powder- used to create a matte appearance

Blush or Rouge- cheek color

Eye Make-up- shadows, liners or mascaras used to define and highlight the eye region

Well groomed eyebrows enhance the eye area and the entire face!

<u>Lip Make-up</u>- liners, gloss and lip colors used to highlight and define the mouth and lip area

Part of your job is to make sure your client knows how to apply their own make-up. You can do a great application, but if they can't duplicate it at home it may be useless to them. If you are doing special occasion make-up, the client may not need to duplicate it in the future. Take the time to explain why you are doing each step and tips on how to apply it. Keep it basic and simple so that the client can apply it themselves.

Make-up is used to both highlight and down play features. Make-up should not be obvious but should enhance the client's own beauty.

Today we are hearing much more about mineral make-up. Whether you've heard of Jane Iredale Mineral Make-up or I.D. Bare Escentuals, mineral make-up it is making a name for itself. If you haven't worked with this before, take the opportunity to learn about this make-up while you are in school. It is becoming much more common and clients are asking about it! You will sound more informed if you ARE more informed about the choices out there!

Quick Tips on Waxing

Waxing is the temporary removal of hair from the skin. It is the process of placing wax on the skin, then removing the hair.

There are many different types of wax: hard wax, soft wax, roll-on wax and resins.

- Clean and dry the area to be waxed.
- Apply wax in the direction of hair growth and remove it against the direction of growth.
- Test the wax's temperature on your inner wrist.
- Never re-use a spatula or "double-dip"
- Wear gloves and practice Universal Precautions
- Always follow through on your pull to cause the least amount of discomfort.
- When you pull the strip off, pull close to the body, rather than up and away.
- Hold the skin taught
- For curly hair, it is important to know what direction the hair is growing in

- Do not wax over the same areas continually, as it will cause skin breakage
- Apply pressure to the newly waxed area directly after pulling the wax or strip off
- Apply a cooling gel after you finish waxing to soothe the waxed area
- Hair should be ¼ to ½ inch long for the best results

Hard wax is applied to the skin with a spatula in a thick layer in the direction of hair growth. When the wax hardens, you flick the end of it to loosen a corner and pull it off with your fingers. Pull against the direction of hair growth. The hair will be attached to the wax that was removed. Hard wax is often used on sensitive areas, but can be a little more costly than soft wax.

Soft wax is applied with a spatula or a roller in a thin layer in the direction of hair growth. Press the pellin or muslin over the wax, pressing it to the wax with the direction of hair growth. Leave a "lip" on the strip to make it easier to grab onto for pulling the strip off.
When you pull the strip off, be sure to follow through and pull close to the body. The hair that was removed will be attached to the pellin with the wax.

There are three hairs in one follicle at any given time:

1. One you can see (telogen)
2. One that is about to come up (catagen)
3. One that you can't see (anagen)

Contraindications:

Do not wax over sunburned skin, on Rosacea, extremely sensitive skin, or on acne.
A client using Retin-A may have thinned skin, as will a client who has just gotten a chemical peel.
Be aware of medications a client may be on that may affect their skin's reaction.

Chapter 7

Peels or Chemical Exfoliation

Esthetics refers to "chemical exfoliations" as "superficial peels", while Doctors "peel" with a medium to deep depth. Be aware of the differences and know when to use which in the appropriate setting.

3 levels of peeling

1. Superficial- only dead cells, AHA, BHA, resorcinol, Microdermabrasion.

2. Medium depth- dermatologist or plastic surgeon, TCA, whole epidermis comes off

3. Deep- medical/surgical- use phenol, remove tissue well into the papillary layer,   controlled chemical burn, laser resurfacing, Dermabrasion- uses rotating wire brush, skin sanding, high concentrations of AHA.

<u>AHA= alpha hydroxy acid</u>

<u>BHA= beta hydroxy acid</u>

<u>AHA-BHA= alpha-beta hydroxy acid</u>

What are the different types of AHA's?

There are different types of AHA's such as glycolic, lactic, tartaric, malic and citric. The most commonly used AHA's used by estheticians are glycolic and lactic acid. It is important to know your state's guidelines on the strength of the peel you are allowed to use and how buffered it needs to be.

What can AHA's do?

AHA's seek out water, break up intercellular cement, and exfoliates the skin.

What does a superficial peel with an AHA feel like?

It feels like a tingling sensation, pinpricks or a itchy feeling. It is normal to experience this feeling and important to let the client know this, so they do not get concerned.

What is a BHA?
BHA stands for Beta Hydroxy Acid

What types of BHA's are there?
Salicylic acid is a BHA. It comes from willow bark, raspberries and wintergreen.

What does a BHA do?
A BHA exfoliates, breaks up oil and sebum and intercellular lipids, and seeks out oil, helps break up congestion in the skin.

What kind of sensations does a client experience with a BHA?
They may smell a strong alcohol smell as well as feeling a "heating up sensation."

What is Alpha-Beta Hydroxy Acid?
Alpha-Beta Hydroxy acid is the marriage of AHA + BHA.
(Example: glycolic + salicylic)
It is good for use on acne/combination skin. You should not use this on very dry or sensitive skin. It is also good for use on hyper pigmentation. This will heat up to the hottest. Be sure your client is aware of what a normal sensation is and what is not.

What is a booster?
A booster is a mixture to boost the strength of a peel.

How often should a client get a peel?
A client will want to make weekly appointments that range from 4-8 weeks. A client should not peel more often than that, and should wait at least 4-6 months before getting another series of peels.

What is a Hayflick Limit?
When the skin is over exfoliated and loses it's ability to bounce back and heal itself properly.

Are there any contraindications to doing a superficial peel?
Yes, you should not do a chemical exfoliation on a client that has chafed or sensitive skin, use using Accutane or RetinA, or is pregnant or lactating.

How can you turn a peel off?
Cool water deactivates it, as do pH
neutralizers. By bringing the pH of the
skin back up it can shut off the peel.
You can also use baking soda with water
to neutralize it.

**What determines the strength of the
peel?**
The percentage of acid along with the pH
factor of the peel determines the
strength. A highly buffered peel that is a
high percentage may not work as well as
a lower percentage peel with a lower pH.

What are some other types of peels?
Check with your state guidelines as to
what you are and are not allowed to use.
Some type of peels can only be used in a
medically supervised setting. It is your
responsibility to know the difference.
Some other types of peels are
Resorcinol, Green Herbal, Obagi Blue
Peel, TCA peels, and Jessner's Peel.

Microdermabrasion

What is Microdermabrasion?
Microdermabrasion is a "sand blasting" of the skin using a self contained unit. You apply crystals to the skin and then vacuum them back up with the machine. It is a form of exfoliation. You will adjust the amount of suction and crystal usage based on the client's skin.

What are the crystals made of?
The crystals are made of aluminum dioxide, corundum or sodium chloride.

What is Microdermabrasion used for?
It is another form of exfoliation. It can be used on all skin types, though you will adjust it for sensitive skin. It is good for sun damage, acne scarring, coarse skin and fine lines.

Are there any contraindications?
Yes, you should not use microdermabrasion on a client that has Rosacea, wounds easily such as a diabetic, a client with inflamed acne, on Accutane, or has extreme sensitivities.

What about consent forms?
You should always have a client sign a consent form when doing microdermabrasion or a superficial peel.

Galvanic and High Frequency

What is the most common modality used during facials?
Galvanic is the most common modality used during facials.

What kind of current does galvanic use?
Galvanic uses DC or direct current.

What is iontophoresis?
It is the introduction of water soluble products to the skin with electricity.

What is cataphoresis?
Cataphoresis forces acidic substances deeper into the skin.

What is Anaphoresis?
Anaphoresis is the process of forcing liquids into the skin.

What do the positive and negative currents do?
Positive closes the pores, negative opens the pores
Positive soothes the nerves, negative stimulates the nerves
Positive decreases the blood supply, negative increases the blood supply
Positive hardens tissue, negative softens tissue

High Frequency is a heat producing current with vibration.

High Frequency can be both direct to the skin and indirect.

High Frequency can also be used to soothe or stimulate the skin.

Charting

Good charting practices and bad charting practices will make a big difference to everyone involved. When you have the knowledge and information to chart properly, everybody will be able to read and understand your charts and will benefit, especially the client.

When charting you may see SOAP notes or CARE notes.

S- Subjective (what the client feels)
O- Objective (what you can actually see)
A- Assessment (what you plan to do and actually carry out)
P- Plan (long term plans: returned visit, use a particular product)

C- Condition of client's skin
A- Action taken, products used
R- Response of client's skin
E- Evaluation of the overall treatment

Some other things you may want to add to the client's chart:

Ask a client what products they are using and note them.
Are they currently happy with the products they are using?
What are the client's sun habits?
Do they wear sun block regularly?
What are the client's areas of concern?
What is the purpose of their visit today?
(Example: deep cleansing or relaxation)
Where do they fall on the Fitzpatrick scale?

OTHER chart things:
- Records are CONFIDENTIAL!
- Beware of legal ramifications
- Date and sign chart, also complete the chart as soon as possible
- Keep in the scope of what you are allowed to do
- Don't speculate!
- Make observations...but DON'T diagnose
- Avoid judgment
- If abbreviating, make sure others can understand
- Sentence fragments are okay if others can understand
- Write the facts, not your feelings
- Write neatly so others can understand
- Allergies or medications

Chapter 8

Licensing, a state decision

Each state sets its own guidelines as to what requirements are needed to get your esthetician license. Every state has its own classroom hour requirements, as well as their own state board testing to acquire your license. After you finish taking your classroom hours, you will be required to take a state certified test. Even if you pass your classroom hours with flying colors, you are not licensed until you pass your state board testing.

For example, in my home state of New Jersey, I am required to sit for 600 hours of classroom and hands on time before being able to take my state board testing. I then have to take a written test and a practical test showing that I know my skills and proper sanitation on the same day.

In the state of Pennsylvania, you are required to sit for 300 hours of classroom and hands on time before taking your state board testing. They take their test on a computer, and then also take a practical test on another date.

My license in New Jersey does not allow me to work in the state of Pennsylvania, just as the esthetician with a license in the state of Pennsylvania is not allowed to work in the state of New Jersey.

How will I know what to do on my test?
Your teacher will prepare you to take your state's test. You may read something that is different from state to state, so be sure to learn what you need to do for your testing.
(Example: some states are allowed to use comedone extractors while others are not)

If I pass my class, do I still have to take a State Board Exam?
Yes, you need to take the State Board Exam to get your license. Your license allows you to work.

What type of questions do they ask on the State Board Exam?
Your state board exam will cover everything you were taught in school from chemistry to sanitation, from facials to electricity, and it may even include your states laws and guidelines.

Will I know what to bring for the practical portion of my test?
Your teacher will prepare you and tell you what items you will need to bring with you.

How long will it take to find out if I passed my test?
Each state will take differing amounts of time.

Do I have to wear uniform or certain items of clothing to take my state board test?
Your teacher will inform you of what you will need to wear.

How long will I have to take my test?
Each state sets its own rules.

How can I find out more information about my state?
Each state is listed with their current information on the following pages.

A

Alabama Esthetician: 1200 hours

Board of Cosmetology
100 North Union St., #320
Montgomery, AL 36130
(334) 242-1918

Alaska Esthetician: 360 hours

Division of Occupational
Licensing Board of Barber & Hairdressers
PO Box 110806
Juneau, AK 99811-0806
(907) 465-2547

Arizona Aesthetician: 600 hours

State Board of Cosmetology
1721 East Broadway Rd.
Tempe, AZ 85282-1611
(480) 784-4539

Arkansas Esthetician: 600 Hours

State Board of Cosmetology
101 F. Capital, Suite 108
Little Rock, AR 72201
(501) 682-2168

C

California Esthetician: 600 hours

Cosmetology Program
PO Box 944226
Sacramento, CA 94244-2260
(916) 445-0713

Colorado Cosmetician: 550 hours

Office of Cosmetologist Licensing
1560 Broadway, #1340
Denver, CO 80202
303.894.7772

Connecticut Esthetics: No **licensing**
for Estheticians until July 1, 2007

Cosmetology & Licensing
410 Capitol Ave., MS #12 APP
P.O. Box 340308
Hartford, CT 06134
(860) 509-7569

D

DC, Washington, DC Skin Care: 125
Hours

Department of Consumer & Regulatory
Affairs
Board of Barbering & Cosmetology
614 H St. N.W., Room 904
Washington, D.C. 20001
(202) 727-7474

Delaware Aesthetician: 300 classroom
hours or 600 apprenticeship hours

Board of Cosmetology &Barbering
Canon Building, #203
PO Box 1401
Dover, DE 19903
(302) 739-4522

F

Florida Skin Care: 260 hours

Department of Business & Professional
Regulation
1940 N. Monroe St.
Tallahassee, FL 32399
(850)-487-1395

G

Georgia Esthetician: 750 Hours,
Apprenticeship 1500

State Board of Cosmetology
237 Coliseum Drive
Macon, GA 31217
(478) 207-1430

H

Hawaii Esthetics: 600 Hours,
apprenticeship 1100 hours

Department of Commerce & Consumer
Affairs
Board of Cosmetology
1010 Richards St.
P.O. Box 3469
Honolulu, HI 96801
(808) 586-3000

I

Idaho Esthetician: 800 hours

Board of Cosmetology
Bureau of Occupational Licenses
Owyhee Plaza
1109 Main St, Suite 220
Boise ID 83702
(208) 334-3233

Illinois Esthetician: 750 hours

Department of Professional Regulation
320 W. Washington St., 3rd Floor,
Springfield, IL 62786
(217) 782-8556

Indiana Esthetician: 700 hours

Professional Licensing Agency
402 W. Washington St., Room W072
Indianapolis, IN 46204
(317) 232-2980

Iowa Esthetician: 600 hours
Department of Public Health

Board of Cosmetology Arts & Sciences
Professional Licensure
Lucas Bldg., 5th Floor
321 E. 12th Street
Des Moines, IA 50319-0075
(515) 281-4416

K

Kansas Esthetics: 650 Hours

State Board of Cosmetology
714 S.W. Jackson
Topeka, KS 66617-1139
(785) 296-3155

Kentucky Esthetician: may be 1000
hours, needed cosmetology license, has
been changes

State Board of Cosmetology
111 St. James Court, #A
Frankfort, KY 40601-2652
(502) 564-4262

L

Louisiana Esthetician: 750 hours

State Board of Cosmetology
11622 Sunbelt Court
Baton Rouge, LA 70809
(225) 756-3404

M

Maine Esthetician: 600 hours

Office of Licensing & Registration
#35 State House Station
Augusta, ME 04333-0035
(207) 624-8579

Maryland Esthetician: 600 hours

State Board of Cosmetologists
500 North Calvert Street, Room 307
Baltimore, MD 21202-3651
(410) 230-6320

Massachusetts Aesthetician: 300 hours

Board of Registration of Cosmetologists
239 Causeway Street, #500
Boston, MA 02114
(617) 727-9940

Michigan Esthetician: 400 hours or 6 months apprenticeship

Bureau of Commercial Services
611 West Ottawa South, North Tower
PO Box 30018
Lansing, MI 48909
(517) 241-9201

Minnesota Esthetician: 600 hours

Department of Commerce
85 7th Place East, #500
Saint Paul, MN 55101
(800) 657-3978

Mississippi Esthetician: 600 hours

State Board of Cosmetology
3000 Old Canton Road, #112
PO Box 55689
Jackson, MS 39296-5689
(601) 987-6837

Missouri Esthetician: 750 hours

State Board of Cosmetology
3605 Missouri Blvd.
PO Box 1062
Jefferson City, MO 65102-1062
(573) 751-1052

Montana Esthetician: 650 hours

Board Barbers and Cosmetologists
301 South Park, 4th Floor
PO Box 200513
Helena, MT 59620-0513
(406) 841-2333

N

Nebraska Esthetician: 600 hours

Department of HHS Regulation and
Licensure
PO Box 95007
Lincoln, NE 68509
(402) 471-2117

Nevada Esthetician: 600 hours

State Board of Cosmetology
1785 East Sahara Avenue, #255
Las Vegas, NV 89104
(702) 486-6542

New Hampshire Esthetician: 600 hours

Board of Barbering Cosmetology &
Esthetics
2 Industrial Park Drive
Concord, NH 03301
(603) 271-3608

New Jersey Skin Care Specialist: 600 hours

Board of Cosmetology and Hairstyling
PO Box 45003
Newark, NJ 07101
(973) 504-6400

New Mexico Esthetician: 600 hours

Board of Barbers & Cosmetologists
2550 Cerrillos Road
Santa Fe, NM 87505
(505) 476-4690

New York Esthetician: 600 hours

Dept of State Division of Licensing
Services
84 Holland Avenue
Albany, NY 12208-3490
(518) 474-4429

North Carolina Esthetician: 600 hours

State Board of Cosmetic Art Examiners
1201 Front Street, #110
Raleigh, NC 27609
(919) 733-4117

North Dakota Esthetician: 600 hours

State Board of Cosmetology
PO Box 2177
Bismarck, ND 58502-2177
(701) 224-9800

O

Ohio Esthetician: 600 hours

State Board of Cosmetology
101 Southland Mall
3700 High Street
Columbus, OH 43207-4041
(614) 466-3834

Oklahoma Esthetician: 600 hours

State Board of Cosmetology
2401 Northwest 23rd Street, #84
Oklahoma City, OK 73107
(405) 521-2441

Oregon Esthetician: 500 hours

Health Licensing Office
700 Summer Street Northeast, #320
Salem, OR 97301-1287
(503) 378-8667

P

Pennsylvania Cosmetician: 300 hours

State Board of Cosmetology
PO Box 2649
Harrisburg, PA 17105-2649
(717) 783-7130

Puerto Rico: 1000 hours, must be
Cosmetologist

Board of Examiners of Beauty Specialists
PO Box 9023271
San Juan, PR 00902-3271
(787) 722-2121

R

Rhode Island Esthetician: 600 hours

Department of Health
3 Capital Hill
Providence, RI 02908
(401) 222-2231

S

South Carolina Esthetician: 450 hours

State Board of Cosmetology
PO Box 11329
Columbia, SC 29211
(803) 896-4568

South Dakota Esthetician: 600 hours

Cosmetology Commission
500 East Capital Avenue
Pierre, SD 57501-5070
(605) 773-6193

T

Tennessee Aesthetician: 750 hours

State Board of Cosmetology
500 James Robertson Parkway
Nashville, TN 37243
(800) 480-9285

Texas Esthetician/Facial Specialist:
600 hours

Cosmetology Commission
5717 Balcones Drive
Austin, TX 78731
(512) 380-7600

U

Utah Esthetician: 600 hours

Division of Occupational & Professional
Licensing
160 East 300 South
Salt Lake City, UT 84114-6741
(801) 530-6628

V

Vermont Esthetician: 600 hours or 12
months of apprenticeship

Office of Professional Regulation
Board of Barbers & Cosmetologists
Redstone Building
26 Terrace Street, Drawer 09
Montpelier, VT 05609-1106
(802) 828-1134

Virginia Esthetician: no license until July 1, 2007, now: cosmetologist 1500 hours

Department of Professional and Occupational Regulation
3600 West Broad Street
Richmond, VA 23230
(804) 367-8509

W

Washington State Esthetician: 600 hours

Department of Licensing
Attn: Cosmetology Unit
PO Box 9026
Olympia, WA 98507-9026
(360) 664-6626

West Virginia Esthetician: 600 hours

State Board of Barbers & Cosmetologists
1716 Pennsylvania Avenue, #7
Charleston, WV 25302
(304) 558-2924

Wisconsin Esthetician: 450 hours

Department of Regulations & Licensing
Barbering & Cosmetology Exam Board
PO Box 8935
Madison, WI 53708-8935
(608) 266-5511

Wyoming Esthetician: 600 hours

Board of Cosmetology
2515 Warren Avenue, #302
Cheyenne, WY 82002
(307) 777-3534

Chapter 9

Extra, extra!

Commonly used abbreviations:

ABCD= asymmetry, border, color, diameter

AHA= alpha hydroxyl acid

ATP= adenosine triphosphate

BHA= beta hydroxyl acid

CARE= condition, action taken, response of skin, evaluation

CDC= center for disease control

CFTA= cosmetic fragrance toiletry association

CRF= cell renewal factor

DHEA= dehydroepiandrosterone

DMAE= dimethylaminoethanol

DNA= deoxyribonucleic acid

EGF= epidermal growth factor

EPA= environmental protection agency

FDA= food and drug administration

FECT= fibro-elastic connective tissue

FGF= fibroblast growth factor

FGP= free gift with purchase

GAG's= glycosaminoglycans

HPIP= history/physical exam, impression, plan

MLD= manual lymph drainage

MSDS= material data safety sheet

NMF= natural moisturizing factor

O/W= oil in water

OSHA- occupational safety and health association

PABA= Para-aminobenzoic Acid

PDR= physician's desk reference

pH= potential hydrogen

RNA= ribonucleic acid

SOAP= subjective, objective, assessment, plan

SPF= sun protection factor

TCA= trichloracetic acid

TEWL= transepidermal water loss

TRF= tissue respiratory factor

TX= treatment

UV= ultraviolet ray

W/O= water in oil

Association Information:

Aesthetics' International Association
(AIA):
2611 N. Belt Line Rd. Suite 101
Sunnyvale, Tx 75182
(800) 961-3777
www.dermascope.com

American Association for Esthetics
Education
401 N. Michigan Ave.
Chicago, IL 60611
(800)648-2505
www.isnow.com

Associated Bodywork and Massage
Professionals
1271 Sugarbush Drive
Evergreen, CO, 80439
(800) 458-2267
www.abmp.com

CIDESCO
National Cosmetology Association,
CIDESCO Section
401 N. Michigan Ave
Suite 2200
Chicago, IL 60611
(312) 527-6765

www.ncacares.org OR www.cidesco.com
International Spa Association (ISPA)
2365 Harrodsburg Rd
Suite A-325
Lexington, KY 40504
(888) 651-4772
www.experienceispa.com

NCEA
484 Spring Avenue, Ridgewood, NJ
07450
Phone: (201) 670-4100
www.ncea.tv

The Day Spa Association
310 17th St
Union City, NJ 07087
(201)865-2065
www.dayspaassociation.com

Trade Shows

What is a trade show?
A trade show is a display of companies who offer product and education for professionals of a particular field. It may be a small show or a very large show.

Who can go to a trade show?
Trade shows are opened to licensed professionals and sometimes students who are studying that profession.

Can students get tickets to trade shows?
Most trade shows offer student priced tickets. Each show sets their rules.

Where can I find out information about trade shows?
Beauty supply stores sometimes have information; trade magazines, professional trade message boards and sometimes you can find one by checking a venues schedule.

Why should I go to a trade show?
You have the opportunity to take extra classes often without an extra fee other than your ticket into the event. It is a great continuing education opportunity. You are also exposed to products you may have not seen or heard of before. It is also a great networking experience.

Can I buy things at a trade show?
Yes, there are many products available for purchase, though some companies will not sell to a student until they have their license.

Do you have any tips about going to my first trade show?
Make a list of the companies you would like to look at, a list of the classes you would like to take and a list of the products you are interested in buying. Get lots of literature to read later. Ask for samples. First time trade show attendees can get caught up in the excitement and spend more money then they had intended. Having a list of your wants will help you stay focused.

Do you have any other tips?
If you stay towards the end of the show, you may find a bargain as the company may rather sell a product than have to pack it up and ship it back. Not all companies do this, but you may get lucky!

Magazine Publications

American Spa Magazine
www.americanspamag.com

BeautyMagOnline.com
www.beautymagonline.com

Day Spa Magazine
www.dayspamagazine.com

Dermascope
www.dermascope.com

Dermasthetic
www.dermasthetic.com

Launchpad
www.beautylaunchpad.com

Les Nouvelles Esthetiques
www.lneonline.com

Make-Up Artist Magazine
www.makeupmag.com

Modern Salon
www.modernsalon.com

Renew (Esthetics Magazine)
www.modernsalon.com

Skin Inc
www.skininc.com

Spa 20/20
www.spa20-20.com

Helpful websites

Delmar Learning (Home of "Milady" books)
www.delmarlearning.com

*Milady also offers an online study and test taking guide. This was invaluable in solidifying what you knew and what you needed to study more.

Aesthetic Video Source
http://www.videoshelf.com/

Look Good...Feel Better
www.lookgoodfeelbetter.org

National Institute on Aging
http://www.nia.nih.gov/

Eyebrow Shaping
http://www.eyebrowz.com/shaping.htm

OneSkin
www.oneskin.com

International Dermal Institute
www.dermalinstitute.com

Anatomy and Skin Research websites:

DermAtlas
http://dermatlas.med.jhmi.edu/derm/

DermNet
www.dermnet.com

Histology of Skin
http://www.vcu.edu/anatomy/OB/Skin~
1/

The Anatomy Lesson
http://mywebpages.comcast.net/wnor/in
dex.htm

Flashcards:

The Amazing Flash Card Machine
www.flashcardmachine.com

Bibliography

Milady's Standard Fundamentals for Estheticians, 9th edition, Delmar Learning

The Clinical Esthetician, Milady's
Delmar Learning

Skin Care Beyond the Basics, Mark Lees
Delmar Learning

Advanced Skin Analysis, Florence Barrett-Hill
Virtual Beauty Corporation, Ltd.

Deborah Schwabe's personal notes

About the Author

Deborah Schwabe resides in the state of NJ. She is both a licensed Skin Care Specialist and Manicurist. After many years in the corporate world, she made a career change and found a new level of satisfaction and enjoyment.